MCAT QUICKSHEETS – PHYSICS

KINEMATICS

Vectors: physical quantities with both magnitude and direction

- Examples: force, velocity

Scalars: physical quantities that have magnitude, but no direction

- Examples: mass, speed

Vector Addition and Subtraction

Tail-to-Tip Method of Finding Resultant of Two Vectors

Finding Resultant Using Component Method

- Resolve vectors into x & y components
- Sum all the vectors in the x direction to get the resultant for the x direction, and do the same for the y components
- The magnitude of the resultant $R = \sqrt{R_x^2 + R_y^2}$

Displacement (Δx): the change in position that goes in a straight-line path from the initial position to the final; it is independent of the path taken (SI unit: m)

Average velocity: $v = \frac{\Delta x}{\Delta t}$ (SI units: m/s)

Acceleration: the rate of change of an object's velocity; it is a vector quantity: $a = \frac{\Delta v}{\Delta t}$ (SI units: m/s²)

Linear Motion

$v = v_0 + at$

$\Delta x = v_0 t + \frac{1}{2}at^2$

$v^2 = v_0^2 + 2a\Delta x$

$v_{avg} = \frac{(v_0 + v)}{2}$

$\Delta x = vt = \left(\frac{v_0 + v}{2}\right)t$

> - When solving for time, there will be two values for t; when the projectile is initially launched and when it impacts the ground.
> - To find max height, remember that the vertical velocity of the projectile is 0 at the highest point of the path.

Projectile Motion

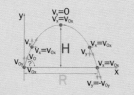

- vertical component of velocity = $v \sin \theta$
- horizontal component of velocity = $v \cos \theta$

Frictional Forces

Static Friction (f_s): is the force that must be overcome to set an object in motion. It has the formula: $0 \leq f_s \leq \mu_s N$

Kinetic Friction (f_k): opposes the motion of objects moving relative to each other. It has the formula: $f_k = \mu_k N$

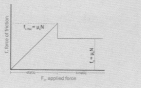

NEWTON'S LAWS

Newton's First Law (Law of Inertia): a body in a state of motion or at rest will remain in that state unless acted upon by a net force

Newton's Second Law: when a net force is applied to a body of mass m, the body will be accelerated in the same direction as the force applied to the mass. This is expressed by the formula $F = ma$ (SI unit: Newton (N) = kg·m/s²).

- $F_{gravity} > F_{parachute}$: person accelerates downward;
- $F_g = F_{parachute}$: terminal velocity is reached (person travels at constant velocity).

Newton's Third Law: if body A exerts a force on body B, then B will exert a force back onto A that is equal in magnitude, but opposite in direction. This can be expressed as, $F_b = -F_a$.

Newton's Law of Gravitation: All forms of matter experience an attractive force to other forms of matter in the universe. The magnitude of the force is represented by: $F = \frac{Gm_1m_2}{r^2}$.

- **Mass (m):** a scalar quantity that measures a body's inertia
- **Weight (W):** a vector quantity that measures a body's gravitational attraction to the earth ($W = mg$)

Uniform Circular Motion:

$a_c = \frac{v^2}{r}$

$F_c = \frac{mv^2}{r}$

center of the circle

Equilibrium

First condition of equilibrium: An object is in translational equilibrium when the sum of forces pushing it one direction is counterbalanced by the sum of forces acting in the opposite direction. It can be expressed as $\sum F = 0$.

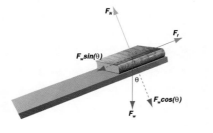

Elastic Collisions – Target at Rest

Conservation of momentum:

$$m_{1i}v_{1i} = m_{1f}v_{1f} + m_{2f}v_{2f}$$

Conservation of kinetic energy:

$$\frac{1}{2}m_{1i}v_{1i}^2 = \frac{1}{2}m_{1f}v_{1f}^2 + \frac{1}{2}m_{2f}v_{2f}^2$$

Impulse $(J) = Ft = \Delta P$

Problem Solving Guide

- Resolve the forces into x and y components.
- $\sum F = 0$ must be true for equilibrium; therefore, $\sum F_x = 0$ and $\sum F_y = 0$.
- Only forces in the x direction affect motion of the object:

$$\sum F_x = ma$$

WORK, ENERGY & MOMENTUM

Work: For a constant force F acting on an object that moves through a distance d, the work is $W = Fd\cos\theta$. (For a force perpendicular to the displacement, $W = 0$.) [SI unit: Joule = N·m]

Power: the rate at which work is performed, and is given by: $P = \frac{W}{t}$ (SI unit: Watt = J/s).

Mechanical Energy

Energy is a scalar quantity (SI unit: Joule).

Kinetic energy: the energy associated with moving objects. It is given by:

$$KE = \frac{1}{2}mv^2$$

Potential energy: the energy associated with a body's position. Gravitational potential energy of an object is due to the force of gravity acting on it, and it is expressed as: $U = mgh$

Total Mechanic Energy

$$E = U + K$$

Mechanical energy is conserved when the sum of kinetic and potential energies remains constant

Work–Energy Theorem

Relates the work performed by all forces acting on a body in a particular time interval to the change in kinetic energy at that time: The expression is:

$$W = \Delta KE$$

Conservation of Energy

When there are no nonconservative forces (e,g., friction) acting on a system, the total mechanical energy remains constant: $\Delta E = \Delta K + \Delta U = 0$

Momentum: a vector quantity. It is given by:

$$p = mv$$

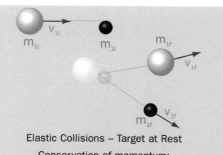

Completely Inelastic Collisions – Target at Rest

	Before	After
Momentum:	$m_1 v_i$	$(m_1 + m_2) v_f$
Kinetic energy:	$\frac{1}{2}m_1 v_i^2$	$\frac{1}{2}(m_1 + m_2) v_f^2$
Conservation of momentum:	$m_1 v_i = (m_1 + m_2)v_f$	

THERMODYNAMICS

Thermal Expansion

Linear Expansion: the increase in length by most solids when heated

Mnemonic: when temperature increases, the length of a solid increases "a Lot"($\alpha L \Delta T$)

$$\Delta L = \alpha L \Delta T$$

Volume Expansion: the increase in volume of fluids when heated

$$\Delta V = \beta V \Delta T$$

Heat Transfer

Conduction: the direct transfer of energy via molecular collisions

Convection: the transfer of heat by the physical motion of the heated material (only liquids and gases)

Radiation: the transfer of energy by electromagnetic waves

Specific Heat

$Q = mc\Delta T$ (Mnemonic: looks like MCAT)

- can only be used to find Q when the object does not change phase
  $Q > 0$ means heat is gained, $Q < 0$ means heat is lost

[SI Units: Joules or calories]

Heat of Transformation: the quantity of heat required to change the **phase** of 1 kg of a substance.

$Q = mL$ (phase changes are isothermal processes)

System Work

- When the piston expands, work is done *by* the system ($W > 0$).
- When the piston compresses the gas, work is done *on* the system ($W < 0$).
- The area under a *P* vs. *V* curve is the amount of work done in a system.

First Law of Thermodynamics: $\Delta U = Q - W$

Process	First Law Becomes
Adiabatic (Q = 0)	$\Delta U = -W$
Constant Volume (W = 0)	$\Delta U = Q$
Closed Cycle (ΔU = 0)	$Q = W$

Second Law of Thermodynamics: in any thermodynamic process that moves from one state of equilibrium to another, the entropy of the system and environment together will either increase or remain unchanged

Elastic Properties of Solids

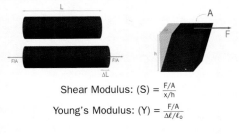

Shear Modulus: $(S) = \frac{F/A}{x/h}$

Young's Modulus: $(Y) = \frac{F/A}{\Delta \ell / \ell_o}$

ELECTROSTATICS

Coulomb's Law

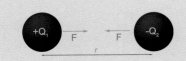

$$F = \frac{kq_1 q_2}{r^2} \text{ [SI units: Newtons]}$$

Electric field

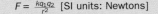

field lines

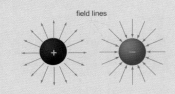

$$E = \frac{F}{q} = \frac{kq}{r^2} \text{ [SI units: N/C or V/m]}$$

- A positive point charge will move in the same direction as the electric field vector; a negative charge will move in the opposite direction.

Electric Potential Energy (U)

The electric potential energy of a charge q at a point in space is the amount of work required to move it from infinity to the point

$$U = q\Delta V = qEd = \frac{kq_1 Q}{r} \text{ [SI units: J]}$$

Electric Dipoles

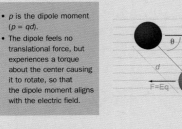

- p is the dipole moment ($p = qd$).
- The dipole feels no translational force, but experiences a torque about the center causing it to rotate, so that the dipole moment aligns with the electric field.

Electric Potential

The amount of work required to move a positive test charge q_o from infinity to a particular point divided by the test charge: $V = \frac{W}{q_o}$ [SI units: Volt = J/C]

Potential Difference (Voltage)

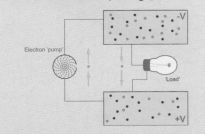

Voltage $(V) = \frac{W}{q} = \frac{kq}{r}$ [SI units: Volt = J/C]

- When two oppositely charged parallel plates are separated by a distance d, an electric field is created, and a potential difference exists between the plates, given by: $V = Ed$.

FLUIDS & SOLIDS

Density $(\rho) = \frac{m}{V}$ [SI units: kg/m^3]

Specific gravity $= \frac{\rho_{substance}}{\rho_{water}}$ [no units]

$$\rho_{water} = 10^3 \text{ kg/m}^3$$

Weight (W) $= \rho g V$

Pressure: a scalar quantity defined as force per unit area: $P = \frac{F}{A}$ [SI units: Pascal = N/m^2]

- For static fluids of uniform density in a sealed vessel, pressure: $P = \rho g h$
- **Absolute pressure** in a fluid due to gravity somewhere below the surface is given by the equation $P = P_o + \rho g h$.
- **Gauge pressure**: $P_g = P_{abs} - P_{environment}$

Continuity Equation: $v_1 A_1 = v_2 A_2$

Bernoulli's Equation: $P + \frac{1}{2}\rho v^2 + \rho g h = $ constant

Archimedes's Principle

$$F_{buoyant} = \rho_{fluid} \, g \, V_{submerged}$$

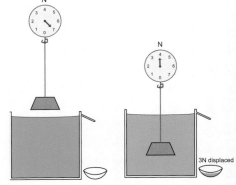

- The buoyant force is equal to the weight of the displaced fluid.
  - If the weight of the fluid displaced is less than the object's weight, then the object will sink.
  - If the weight of the fluid displaced by the object is greater than or equal to object's weight, then it will float.

Pascal's Principle

- A change in the pressure applied to an enclosed fluid is transmitted undiminished to every portion of the fluid and to the walls of the containing vessel.

$$\Delta P = \frac{F_1}{A_1} = \frac{F_2}{A_2} \text{ and } A_1 d_1 = A_2 d_2$$
$$\text{so, } W = F_1 d_1 = F_2 d_2$$

MAGNETISM

The Magnetic Field (B)

Magnetic fields are created by permanent magnets and moving charges

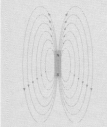

Magnetic field lines depict the direction a compass needle would point if placed in the field from the North Pole to the South Pole [SI Units = Tesla(T) = N·s/m·C]

Force on a Moving Charge

A charge moving in a magnetic field experiences a force exerted on it.

$$F = qvB\sin\theta$$

The magnetic force is zero when charges move parallel or antiparallel to the magnetic field

Right-Hand Rule For Finding Direction of Force

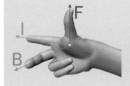

Note that the right-hand rule gives the direction of magnetic force exerted on a proton. The direction of force on an electron is simply in the opposite direction of the force on a proton.

Force on a Current-Carrying Wire

$$F = iLB\sin\theta$$

X → represents B fields pointing into the page,
• → represents B fields pointing out of the page.

Special Cases

Center of Wire Loop
$$B = \frac{\mu_0 i}{2r}$$

Around a Straight Wire
$$B = \frac{\mu_0 i}{2\pi r}$$

Right-Hand Rule for Direction of B Field produced by Current-Carrying Wires

- Right thumb points in the direction of current flow
- Wrap your fingers around the wire as if you were grabbing it with your palm
- The direction that the fingers curl is the direction of the magnetic field

Wave Superposition

Constructive

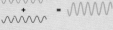

Waves can also be shifted with respect to one another by other fractions of a cycle, such as $\frac{1}{4}\lambda$, or 90° out of phase.

Destructive

DC AND AC CIRCUITS

Direct Current

Current: the flow of electric charge. Current is given by:

$I = \frac{\Delta q}{\Delta t}$ [SI units: Amp (A) = C/s]

(The direction of current is the direction positive charge would flow, or from high to low potential.)

Ohm's Law and Resistance

$V = IR$ (can be applied to entire circuit or individual resistors)

Resistance: opposition to the flow of charge.
$R = \frac{\rho L}{A}$ (Resistance increases with increasing temperatures with most conductors)
[SI Units: Ohm (Ω)]

Circuit Laws

Kirchoff's Laws:

1. At any junction within a circuit, the sum of current flowing into that point must equal the current leaving

2. The sum of voltage sources equals the sum of voltage drops around a closed circuit loop

Alternating current

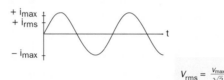

$$V_{rms} = \frac{V_{max}}{\sqrt{2}}$$

$$I_{rms} = \frac{I_{max}}{\sqrt{2}}$$

Series Circuits

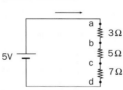

$R_{eff} = R_1 + R_2 + R_3...$
$V_{eff} = V_1 + V_2 + V_3...$
$I_{eff} = I_1 = I_2 = I_3...$

Parallel Circuits

$1/R_{eff} = 1/R_1 + 1/R_2 + 1/R_3$
$V_{eff} = V_1 = V_2 = V_3 = ...$
$I_{eff} = I_1 + I_2 + I_3 + ...$

Power Dissipated by Resistors

$$P = IV = \frac{V^2}{R} = I^2R$$

Capacitors

Capacitance: the ability to store charge per unit voltage. It is given by: $C = \frac{Q}{V}$

$$C = \kappa \frac{\varepsilon_0 A}{d}$$

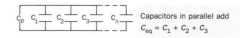

Capacitors in parallel add
$C_{eq} = C_1 + C_2 + C_3$

Energy stored by Capacitors:

$$U = \frac{1}{2}QV = \frac{1}{2}CV^2 = \frac{1}{2}Q^2/C$$

PERIODIC MOTION AND WAVES

Simple Harmonic Motion

Force in a Spring $(F) = -k\bar{x}$
Potential Energy of Spring $(U) = \frac{1}{2}kx^2$

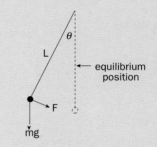

← equilibrium position

Total Energy $(E) = K + U = \frac{1}{2}kA^2$

	mass-spring	Simple pendulum
Force constant (k)	Spring constant (k)	mg/L
ang. freq. ω	$\sqrt{\frac{k}{m}}$	$\sqrt{\frac{g}{L}}$
frequency f	$\frac{1}{T}$ or $\frac{\omega}{2\pi}$	$\frac{1}{T}$ or $\frac{\omega}{2\pi}$
Kinetic energy K	$\frac{1}{2}mv^2$	$\frac{1}{2}mv^2$
K_{max} occurs at	$x = 0$	$\theta = 0$ (vertical position)
potential energy U	$\frac{1}{2}kx^2$	mgh
U_{max} occurs at	$x = \pm x$	Max value of θ
max acceleration	$x = \pm x$	Max value of θ

Describing Waves

Longitudinal Wave

Transverse Wave

Wave Formulas

$$f = \frac{1}{T}$$

$$v = f\lambda$$

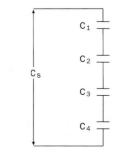

Capacitors in series add as reciprocals

$\frac{1}{C_{eq}} = \frac{1}{C_1} + \frac{1}{C_2} + \frac{1}{C_3}...$

SOUND

Sound propagates through a deformable medium by the oscillation of particles along the direction of the wave's motion.

Intensity (I) = P/A [SI units: W/m^2]

Sound Level (β) = $10 \log (I/I_o)$ [unit: decibel = $d\beta$]

(Note that an increase in intensity by a factor of 100, for instance 40 W/m^2 to 4,000 W/m^2, corresponds to an increase of 20 $d\beta$)

Beats occur when two waves that have slightly different frequencies are superimposed:

$f_{beat} = |f_1 - f_2|$

Standing Waves

Strings

$\lambda = \frac{2L}{n}$ ($n = 1, 2, 3...$)

$f = \frac{nv}{2L}$ ($n = 1, 2, 3...$)

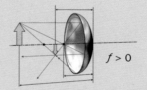

The ends of the strings are always nodes.

Open Pipes

$\lambda = \frac{2L}{n}$ ($n = 1, 2, 3...$)

$f = \frac{nv}{2L}$ ($n = 1, 2, 3...$)

$L = \frac{\lambda}{2}$

$L = \lambda$

$L = \frac{3\lambda}{2}$

The open ends of the pipes are always antinodes (max amplitude). Nodes occur where the displacement is zero.

Closed Pipes

$\lambda = \frac{4L}{n}$ ($n = 1, 3, 5...$)

$f = \frac{nv}{4L}$ ($n = 1, 3, 5...$)

(odd integers only)

$L = \frac{\lambda}{4}$

$L = \frac{3\lambda}{4}$

$L = \frac{5\lambda}{4}$

The closed end of the pipe is always a node, and the open end is always an antinode.

Refraction

$n = \frac{c}{v}$ (speed of light = 3×10^8 m/s)

Snell's Law: $n_1 \sin \theta_1 = n_2 \sin \theta_2$ when $n_2 > n_1$, light bends toward normal, when $n_2 < n_1$, light bends away from normal

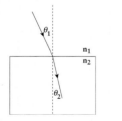

Diffraction

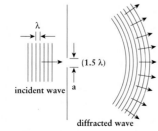

To locate dark fringes, use the formula:

$a \sin \theta = n\lambda$ ($n = 1, 2, 3...$)

Doppler Effect

- When a source and a detector move relative to one another, the perceived frequency of the sound received differs from the actual frequency emitted even though the source velocity and frequency is unchanged

$$f' = f \frac{(v \pm v_D)}{(v \mp v_S)}$$

Stationary source: $V_s = 0$

Stationary detector: $V_d = 0$

Observer and detector moving closer:
- "+" sign in numerator
- "−" sign in denominator

Observer and detector moving apart:
- "−" sign in numerator
- "+" sign in denominator

OPTICS

Spherical Mirrors

Mirror Equation: $\frac{1}{i} + \frac{1}{o} = \frac{1}{f} = \frac{2}{r}$

- Any of units of distance may be used, but all units used must be the same.

Concave Mirrors

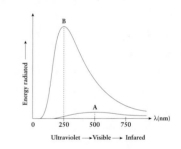

- If an object is placed inside the focal length of a concave mirror, the image formed is behind the mirror, enlarged and virtual.

Convex Mirrors

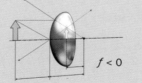

- Regardless of the position of the object, a convex mirror forms only a virtual erect image.

Thin Spherical Lenses

Lens Equation: $\frac{1}{f} = \frac{1}{o} + \frac{1}{i}$

Converging Lenses

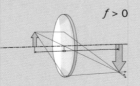

- For an object beyond the focal point, the image formed is real and inverted.
- For an object inside the focal length, the image formed is virtual, erect and enlarged.
- No image at focal point.

Diverging Lenses

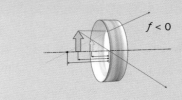

Magnification (m) = $\frac{-i}{o}$

- $|m| < 1$ image reduced; $|m| > 1$ image enlarged; $|m| = 1$ image same size
- Inverted image has a negative m, erect image has a positive m.

ATOMIC AND NUCLEAR PHENOMENA

Blackbody Radiation

A **blackbody** is an object that absorbs all incident electromagnetic radiation upon it and emits energy that is characteristic to the system itself

Wien's Displacement Law: $\lambda_{peak}T$ = constant

Stefan-Boltzmann Law: $E_{total} = \sigma T^4$

Photoelectric Effect

$E = hf = \frac{hc}{\lambda}$

$K = hf - W$

K is the maximum kinetic energy of ejected electron; W is the minimum energy required to eject an electron).

Nuclear Binding Energy

Mass defect: the difference between the sum of the masses of nucleons in the nucleus and the mass of the nucleus. The mass defect results from the conversion of matter to energy, embodied by: $E = mc^2$. This energy is the **binding energy** that holds nucleons within the nucleus.

Exponential Decay

Half Life
$n = n_o\ e^{-\lambda t}$

Alpha decay
$^{238}_{92}U \rightarrow ^{234}_{90}Th + ^{4}_{2}He$

Beta Minus Decay
$^{137}_{55}Cs \rightarrow ^{137}_{56}Ba + ^{0}_{-1}e^- + \bar{v}_e$

Beta Plus Decay
$^{22}_{11}Na \rightarrow ^{22}_{10}Ne + ^{0}_{+1}e^+ + v_e$

ATOMIC STRUCTURE

Atomic weight: the weight in grams of one mole (mol) of a given element and is expressed in terms of g/mol.

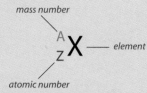

mass number

$$_Z^A X$$ — *element*

atomic number

A **mole** is a unit used to count particles and is represented by **Avogadro's number**, 6.022×10^{23} particles.

$$\text{Moles} = \frac{\text{grams}}{\text{atomic or molecular weight}}$$

Isotopes: For a given element, multiple species of atoms with the same number of protons (same atomic number) but different numbers of neutrons (different mass numbers).

Planck's quantum theory: Energy emitted as electromagnetic radiation from matter exists in discrete bundles called quanta.

Bohr's Model of the Hydrogen Atom

Angular momentum $= \frac{nh}{2\eta}$

Energy of electron $= E = \frac{-R_H}{n^2}$

Electromagnetic energy of photons $= E = \frac{hc}{\lambda}$

The group of hydrogen emission lines corresponding to transitions from upper levels $n > 2$ to $n = 2$ is known as the **Balmer series**, while the group corresponding to transitions between upper levels $n > 1$ to $n = 1$ is known as the **Lyman series**.

Absorption spectrum: Characteristic energy bands where electrons absorb energy.

Quantum Mechanical Model of Atoms

Heisenberg uncertainty principle: It is impossible to determine with perfect accuracy the momentum and the position of an electron simultaneously.

Quantum Numbers:

#	Character	Symbol	Value
1st	Shell	n	n
2nd	Subshell	l	From zero to n–1
3rd	Orbital	m_ℓ	Between l and –l
4th	Spin	m_s	½ or –½

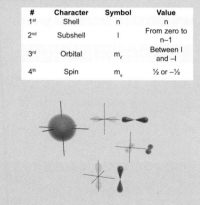

Principal Quantum Number (*n*): The larger the integer value of *n*, the higher the energy level and radius of the electron's orbit. The maximum number of electrons in energy level *n* is $2n^2$.

Azimuthal Quantum Number (*l*): Refers to subshells, or sublevels. The four subshells corresponding to *l* = 0, 1, 2, and 3 are known as s, p, d and f, respectively. The maximum number of electrons that can exist within a subshell is given by the equation $4l+2$.

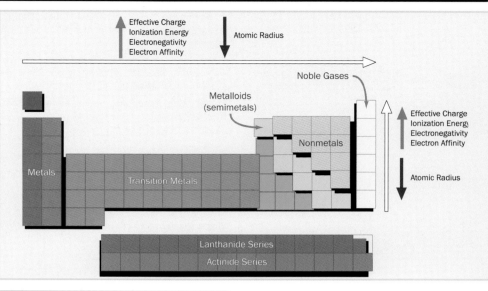

BONDING & CHEMICAL INTERACTIONS

Octet rule:

- atom will bond until it has a full outermost shell
- atom wants to have a configuration similar to that of Group VII (noble gases)
- exceptions: H, Li, Be, B, P, and S.

Exceptions: Atoms found in or beyond the third period can have more than eight valence electrons, since some of the valence electrons may occupy d orbitals. These atoms can have more than four bonds in Lewis structures.

For instance, the sulfate ion can be drawn in six resonance forms, each with the two double bonds attached to a different combination of oxygen atoms.

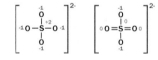

Magnetic Quantum Number (m_l): This specifies the particular orbital within a subshell where an electron is highly likely to be found at a given point in time.

Spin Quantum Number (m_s): The spin of a particle is its intrinsic angular momentum and is a characteristic of a particle, like its charge.

Electron Configuration

Hund's rule: Within a given subshell, orbitals are filled such that there are a maximum number of half-filled orbitals with parallel spins.

Valence electrons: Electrons of an atom that are in its outer energy shell or that are available for bonding.

Covalent Bond Notation

Lewis Structures: The chemical symbol of an element surrounded by dots, each representing one of the s and/or p valence electrons of the atom

Steps for drawing Lewis Structures:

1. Write the skeletal structure of the compound.

    H–C–N

2. Count all the valence electrons of the atoms.

3. Draw single bonds between the central atom and the atoms surrounding it.

    H : C : N

4. Complete the octets of all atoms bonded to the central atom, using the remaining valence electrons still to be assigned.

    H : C : N̈ :

5. Place any extra electrons on the central atom.

    H – C ≡ N

Formal Charges

Formal charge =
    Valence electrons $- \frac{1}{2} N_{\text{bonding}} - N_{\text{nonbonding}}$

Geometry and Polarity of Covalent Molecules

Polar Covalent Bond: Bonding electron pair is not shared equally, but pulled towards more electronegative atom.

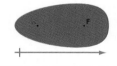

Polarity of Molecules: Depends on the polarity of the constituent bonds and on the shape of the molecule. A molecule with nonpolar bonds is always nonpolar; a molecule with polar bonds may be polar or nonpolar depending on the orientation of the bond dipoles.

The overall shape of the molecule determines whether the molecule is in fact polar or not. For instance, the four bond dipoles for the CCl_4 molecule point to the vertices of the tetrahedron and cancel each other.

no net dipole moment

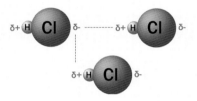

Regions of electron density	Example	Geometric arrangement of electron pairs around the central atom	Shape	Angle between electron pairs
2	$BeCl_2$	X — H — X	linear	180°
3	BH_3		trigonal planar	120°
4	CH_4		tetrahedral	109.5°
5	PCl_5		trigonal bipyramidal	90°, 120°, 180°
6	SF_6		octahedral	90°, 180°

Intermolecular Forces

1. **Dipole-Dipole Interactions**: Polar molecules orient themselves such that the positive region of one molecule is close to the negative region of another molecule.

2. **Hydrogen Bonding**: The partial positive charge of the hydrogen atom interacts with the partial negative charge located on the electronegative atoms (F, O, N) of nearby molecules.

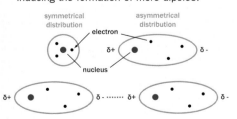

3. **Dispersion Forces**: The bonding electrons in covalent bonds may appear to be equally shared between two atoms, but at any particular point in time they will be located randomly throughout the orbital. This permits unequal sharing of electrons, causing rapid polarization and counter-polarization of the electron clouds of neighboring molecules, inducing the formation of more dipoles.

symmetrical distribution — electron — asymmetrical distribution — nucleus — $\delta+$ — $\delta-$

COMPOUNDS & STOICHIOMETRY

A **compound** is a pure substance that is composed of two or more elements in a fixed proportion.

A **mole** is the amount of a substance that contains the same number of particles that are found in a 12.000 g sample of carbon-12.

Combination Reactions: two or more reactants form one product.

$$S\ (s) + O_2\ (g) \rightarrow SO_2\ (g)$$

Decomposition Reactions: a compound breaks down into two or more substances, usually as a result of heating or electrolysis.

$$2HgO\ (s) \rightarrow 2Hg\ (l) + O_2\ (g)$$

Single Displacement Reactions: an atom (or ion) of one compound is replaced by an atom of another element.

$$Zn\ (s) + CuSO_4\ (aq) \rightarrow Cu\ (s) + ZnSO_4\ (aq)$$

Double Displacement Reactions: also called metathesis reactions, elements from two different compounds displace each other to form two new compounds.

$$CaCl_2\ (aq) + 2\ AgNO_3\ (aq) \rightarrow$$
$$Ca(NO_3)_2\ (aq) + 2\ AgCl\ (s)$$

Net Ionic Equations: These types of equations are written showing only the species that actually participate in the reaction. So in the following equation,

$$Zn\ (s) + Cu^{2+}\ (aq) + SO_4^{2-}\ (aq) \rightarrow$$
$$Cu\ (s) + Zn^{2+}\ (aq) + SO_4^{2-}\ (aq)$$

The spectator ion (SO_4^{2-}) does not take part in the overall reaction, but simply remains in solution throughout. The net ionic equation would be:

$$Zn\ (s) + Cu^{2+}\ (aq) \rightarrow Cu\ (s) + Zn^{2+}\ (aq)$$

Neutralization Reactions: These are a specific type of double displacements which occur when an acid reacts with a base to produce a solution of a salt and water:

$$HCl\ (aq) + NaOH\ (aq) \rightarrow NaCl\ (aq) + H_2O\ (l)$$

KINETICS & EQUILIBRIUM

Experimental Determination of Rate Law: The values of k, x, and y in the rate law equation (rate = $k\ [A]^x\ [B]^y$) must be determined experimentally for a given reaction at a given temperature. The rate is usually measured as a function of the initial concentrations of the reactants, A and B.

Efficiency of Reactions

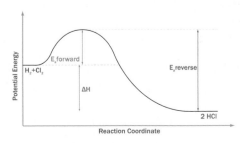

Factors affecting reaction rates: Reactant Concentrations, Temperature, Medium, Catalysts

Catalysts are unique substances that increase reaction rate without being consumed; they do this by lowering the activation energy.

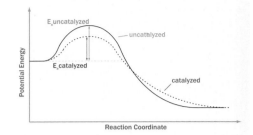

Law of Mass Action

$$a\ A + b\ B \rightleftharpoons c\ C + d\ D$$

$$K_C = \frac{[C]^c[D]^d}{[A]^a[B]^b}$$

K_C is the equilibrium constant. (c stands for concentration.)

Properties of The Equilibrium Constant

Pure solids/liquids don't appear in expression

K_{eq} is characteristic of a given system at a given temperature

If $K_{eq} \gg 1$, an equilibrium mixture of reactants and products will contain very little of the reactants compared to the products.

If $K_{eq} \ll 1$, an equilibrium mixture of reactants and products will contain very little of the products compared to the reactants.

If K_{eq} is close to 1, an equilibrium mixture of products and reactants will contain approximately equal amounts of the two.

Le Châtelier's principle is used to determine the direction in which a reaction at equilibrium will proceed when subjected to a stress, such as a change in concentration, pressure, temperature, or volume. The key is to remember that a system to which these kinds of stresses are applied tends to change so as to relieve the applied stress.

In a Nutshell:

A + B $\rightleftharpoons$ C + heat	
Will shift to **RIGHT**	Will shift to **LEFT**
1. if more A or B added	1. if more C added
2. if C taken away	2. if A or B taken away
3. if pressure applied or volume reduced (assuming A, B, and C are gases)	3. if pressure reduced or volume increased (assuming A, B, and C are gases)
4. if temperature reduced	4. if temperature increased

THERMOCHEMISTRY

The Law of Conservation of Energy dictates that all thermal, chemical, potential, and kinetic energies are interconvertible.

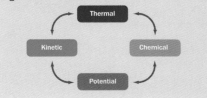

Systems:

isolated: no exchange of energy/matter

closed: exchange energy but not matter

open: can exchange both energy and matter

System Processes:

isothermal: temp of system remains constant

adiabatic: no heat exchange occurs

isobaric: pressure of system remains constant

Heat: A form of energy which can easily transfer to or from a system.

endothermic: rxns that absorb heat energy

exothermic: rxns that release heat energy

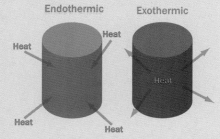

Endothermic   Exothermic

Constant-volume and constant-pressure calorimetry: used to indicate conditions under which the heat changes are measured.

$q = mc\triangle T$, where q is the heat absorbed or released in a given process, m is the mass, c is the specific heat, and $\triangle T$ is the change in temperature.

States and State Functions: are described by the macroscopic properties of the system. These are properties whose magnitude depends only on the initial and final states of the system, and not on the path of the change.

Enthalpy (H): is used to express heat changes at constant pressure.

Standard Heat of Formation ($\triangle H°_f$): the enthalpy change that would occur if one mole of a compound were formed directly from its elements in their standard states.

Standard Heat of Reaction ($\triangle H°_{rxn}$): the hypothetical enthalpy change that would occur if the reaction were carried out under standard conditions.

$\triangle H°_{rxn}$ = (sum of $\triangle H°_{rxn}$ of products) − (sum of $\triangle H°_{rxn}$ of reactants)

Hess's Law: states that enthalpies of reactions are additive.

The reverse of any reaction has an enthalpy of the same magnitude as that of the forward reaction, but its sign is opposite.

Bond Dissociation Energy: an average of the energy required to break a particular type of bond in one mole of gaseous molecules:

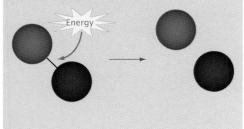

Energy

---

1 atm = 760 mm Hg = 760 torr

Do not confuse STP with standard conditions—the two standards involve different temperatures and are used for different purposes. STP (0°C or 273 K) is generally used for gas law calculations; standard conditions (25°C or 298 K) is used when measuring standard enthalpy, entropy, Gibbs free energy, and voltage.

Boyle's Law

$$PV = k \text{ or } P_1V_1 = P_2V_2$$

Law of Charles and Gay-Lussac

$$\frac{V}{T} = k \text{ or } \frac{V_1}{T_1} = \frac{V_2}{T_2}$$

Avagadro's Principle

$$\frac{n}{V} = k \text{ or } \frac{n_1}{V_1} = \frac{n_2}{V_2}$$

Ideal Gas Law

$$PV = nRT$$

Real Gases

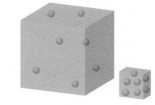

Decreasing the volume of a sample of gas makes it behave more like a real gas since the individual gas particles are in closer proximity in a smaller volume. (They are more likely to engage in intermolecular interactions.)

Entropy (S): the measure of the disorder, or randomness, of a system.

$$\triangle S_{universe} = \triangle S_{system} + \triangle S_{surroundings}$$

Gibbs Free Energy (G): combines the two factors which affect the spontaneity of a reaction—changes in enthalpy, $\triangle H$, and changes in entropy, $\triangle S$.

$$\triangle G = \triangle H - T\triangle S$$

if $\triangle G$ is negative, the rxn is spontaneous

if $\triangle G$ is positive, the rxn is not spontaneous

if $\triangle G$ is zero, the system is in a state of equilibrium; thus, $\triangle G = 0$ and $\triangle H = T\triangle S$

ΔH	ΔS	Outcome
−	+	Spontaneous at all temps.
+	−	Nonspontaneous at all temps.
+	+	Spontaneous only at high temps.
−	−	Spontaneous only at low temps.

Reaction Quotient (Q): Once a reaction commences, the standard state conditions no longer hold. For the reaction,

$$a A + b B \rightleftharpoons c C + d D$$

$$Q = \frac{[C]^c[D]^d}{[A]^a[B]^b}$$

Deviations due to Pressure: As the pressure of a gas increases, the particles are pushed closer and closer together. At moderately high pressure a gas' volume is less than would be predicted by the ideal gas law, due to intermolecular attraction.

Deviations due to Temperature: As the temperature of a gas decreases, the average velocity of the gas molecules decreases, and the attractive intermolecular forces become increasingly significant. As the temperature of a gas is reduced, intermolecular attraction causes the gas to have a smaller volume than would be predicted.

Van Der Waals Equation of State: accounts for the deviations from ideality which occur when a gas does not closely follow the ideal gas law.

$$(P + \frac{n^2a}{V^2})(V - nb) = nRT$$

1 mole of gas at STP = 22.4 L

Dalton's Law of Partial Pressures: This law states that the total pressure of a gaseous mixture is equal to the sum of the partial pressures of the individual components.

$$P_T = P_A + P_B + P_C + ...$$
$$P_A = P_TX_A$$

Where $X_A = \frac{n_A}{n_T}$ $\frac{\text{(moles of A)}}{\text{(total moles)}}$

Kinetic Molecular Theory of Gases: An explanation of gaseous molecular behavior based on the motion of individual molecules.

Average Molecular Speeds

$$KE = \frac{1}{2}mv^2 = \frac{3}{2}kT$$

Root-mean-square speed

$$U_{rms} = (\frac{3RT}{MM})^{\frac{1}{2}}$$

---

simple cubic   body-centered cubic   face-centered cubic

pressure / temperature phase diagram: Solid, Liquid, Gas, triple point, critical point

Colligative Properties: These are physical properties derived solely from the number of particles present, not the nature of those particles. These properties are usually associated with dilute solutions.

Freezing Point Depression

$$\triangle T_f = K_f m$$

Boiling Point Elevation

$$\triangle T_b = K_b m$$

Osmotic Pressure

$$\Pi = MRT$$

Vapor-pressure Lowering (Raoult's Law)

$$P_A = X_A P^\circ_A;\ P_B = X_B P^\circ_B$$

Solutions that obey Raoult's Law are called ideal solutions.

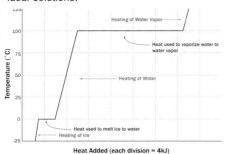

Heat Added (each division = 4kJ)

Graham's Law of Diffusion and Effusion

Diffusion: occurs when gas molecules diffuse through a mixture.

Effusion: is the flow of gas particles under pressure from one compartment to another through a small opening.

Effusion

Both diffusion and effusion have the same formula: $\frac{r_1}{r_2} = \left(\frac{MM_2}{MM_1}\right)^{\frac{1}{2}}$

SOLUTIONS

1. All salts of alkali metals are water soluble.
2. All salts of the ammonium ion (NH_4^+) are water soluble.
3. All chlorides, bromides, and iodides are water soluble, with the exceptions of Ag^+, Pb^{2+}, and Hg^{2+}.
4. All salts of the sulfate ion (SO_4^{2-}) are water soluble, with the exceptions of Ca^{2+}, Sr^{2+}, Ba^{2+}, and Pb^{2+}.
5. All metal oxides are insoluble, with the exception of the alkali metals and CaO, SrO, BaO, all of which hydrolyze to form solutions of the corresponding metal hydroxides.
6. All hydroxides are insoluble, with the exception of the alkali metals and Ca^{2+}, Sr^{2+}, and Ba^{2+}.
7. All carbonates (CO_3^{2-}), phosphates (PO_4^{3-}), sulfides (S^{2-}), and sulfites (SO_3^{2-}) are insoluble, with the exception of the alkali metals and ammonium.

Units of Concentration

Percent Composition by Mass:

$= \frac{\text{Mass of solute}}{\text{Mass of solution}} \times 100\ (\%)$

Mole Fraction: $\frac{\text{\# of mol of compound}}{\text{total \# of moles in system}}$

Molarity: $\frac{\text{\# of mol of solute}}{\text{liter of solution}}$

Molality: $\frac{\text{\# of mol of solute}}{\text{kg of solvent}}$

Normality: $\frac{\text{\# of gram equivalent weights of solute}}{\text{liter of solution}}$

ACIDS AND BASES

Arrhenius Definition: An acid is a species that produces H^+ (a proton) in an aqueous solution, and a base is a species that produces OH^- (a hydroxide ion).

Bronsted-Lowry Definition: An acid is a species that donates protons, while a base is a species that accepts protons.

Lewis Definition: An acid is an electron-pair acceptor, and a base is an electron-pair donor.

Properties of Acids and Bases

$$pH = -\log[H^+] = \log\left(\frac{1}{[H^+]}\right)$$

$$pOH = -\log[OH^-] = \log\left(\frac{1}{[OH^-]}\right)$$

$$H_2O(l) \rightleftharpoons H^+(aq) + OH^-(aq)$$

$$K_w = [H^+][OH^-] = 10^{-14}$$

$$pH + pOH = 14$$

Weak Acids and Bases

$$HA\ (aq) + H_2O\ (l) \rightleftharpoons H_3O^+\ (aq) + A^-\ (aq)$$

$$K_a = \frac{[H_3O^+][A^-]}{[HA]}$$

$$K_b = \frac{[B^+][OH^-]}{[BOH]}$$

Salt Formation: Acids and bases may react with each other, forming a salt and (often, but not always) water in a neutralization reaction.

$$HA + BOH \rightarrow BA + H_2O$$

Hydrolysis: This is the reverse reaction, where the salt ions react with water to give back the acid and base.

Amphoteric Species: is one that can act either as an acid or a base, depending on its chemical environment.

Titration and Buffers

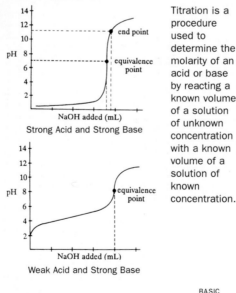

Strong Acid and Strong Base

Weak Acid and Strong Base

Titration is a procedure used to determine the molarity of an acid or base by reacting a known volume of a solution of unknown concentration with a known volume of a solution of known concentration.

Henderson-Hasselbalch equation is used to estimate the pH of a solution in the buffer region where the concentrations of the species and its conjugate are present in approximately equal concentrations.

$$pH = pK_a + \log\frac{[\text{conjugate base}]}{[\text{weak acid}]}$$

$$pOH = pK_b + \log\frac{[\text{conjugate acid}]}{[\text{weak base}]}$$

BASIC

NaOH
NH3
HCO3
F⁻
Water
H2CO3
NH4⁺
HSO4
HF
HCl

ACIDIC

REDOX REACTIONS & ELECTROCHEMISTRY

Oxidation: loss of electrons

Reduction: gain of electrons

Oxidizing agent: causes another atom to undergo oxidation, and is itself reduced.

Reducing agent: causes another atom to be reduced, and is itself oxidized.

Galvanic Cells

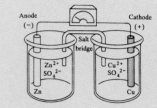

A redox reaction occurring in a galvanic cell has a negative $\triangle G$ and is therefore a spontaneous reaction. Galvanic cell reactions supply energy and are used to do work.

This energy can be harnessed by placing the oxidation/reduction half-reactions in separate containers called half-cells. The half-cells are then connected by an apparatus that allows for the flow of electrons.

Electrolytic Cells

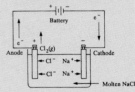

A redox reaction occurring in an electrolytic cell has a positive $\triangle G$ and is therefore nonspontaneous. In electrolysis, electrical energy is required to induce reaction. The oxidation and reduction half reactions are usually placed in one container.

Reduction potential of each species is defined as the tendency of a species to acquire electrons and be reduced. Standard reduction potential, (E°) is measured under standard conditions: 25°C, 1 M concentration for each ion in the reaction, a partial pressure of 1 atm for each gas and metals in their pure state.

Standard reduction potentials are used to calculate the standard electromotive force (EMF or E°_{cell}) of a reaction, the difference in potential between two half-cells.

$$EMF = E^\circ_{red} + E^\circ_{ox}$$

Gibbs free energy, $\triangle G$, is the thermodynamic criterion for determining the spontaneity of a reaction.

$$\triangle G = -nFE_{cell}$$

NOMENCLATURE

1. Find the longest carbon chain containing the principle functional group (highest priority groups are generally more oxidized).
2. Number the carbon chain so that the principle functional group gets lowest number (1).
3. Proceed to number the chain so that the lowest set of numbers is obtained for the substituents.
4. Name the substituents and assign each a number.
5. Complete the name by listing substituents in alphabetical order, place commas between numbers and dashes between numbers and words.

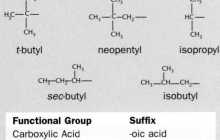

t-butyl   neopentyl   isopropyl

sec-butyl   isobutyl

Functional Group	Suffix
Carboxylic Acid	-oic acid
Ester	-oate
Acyl halide	-oyl halide
Amide	-amide
Nitrile/Cyanide	-nitrile
Aldehyde	-al
Ketone	-one
Thiol	-thiol
Alcohol	-ol
Amine	-amine
Imine	-imine
Ether	-ether

ALKANES

1° → CH_3
3°
2°

Free radical halogenation
- Initiation
- Propagation
- Termination

Combustion
$$C_3H_8 + 5O_2 \rightarrow 3CO_2 + 4H_2O + heat$$

Nucleophilicity and Basicity
$$RO^- > HO^- > RCO_2^- > ROH > H_2O$$

Nucleophilicity, size, and polarity
$$CN^- > I^- > RO^- > HO^- > Br^- > Cl^- > F^- > H_2O$$

Leaving groups (weak bases best)
$$I^- > Br^- > Cl^- > F^-$$

	S_N1	S_N2
	2 steps	1 step
	Favored in polar protic solvents	Favored in polar aprotic solvents
	3° > 2° > 1° > methyl	Methyl > 1° > 2° > 3°
	Rate = k[RX]	Rate = k[Nu][RX]
	Racemic products	Optically active and inverted products
	Strong nucleophile not required	Favored with strong nucleophile

BONDING

Bond order	single	double	triple
Bond type	sigma	sigma	sigma
		pi	2 pi
Hybridization	sp^3	sp^2	sp
Angles	109.5°	120°	180°
Example	C–C	C=C	C≡C

ISOMERS

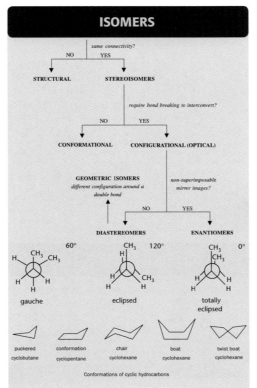

Conformations of cyclic hydrocarbons

ALKYNES

Alkynes have a terminal hydrogen that is appreciably more acidic than hydrogens on alkanes and alkenes.

Synthesis via double elimination of geminal or vicinal dihalide

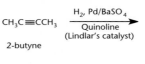

$$CH_3C{\equiv}CCH_3 + 2HBr$$

Oxidation with $KMnO_4$, O_3

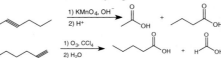

Reduction with Lindlar's Catalyst or liquid ammonia

$CH_3C{\equiv}CCH_3$ →(H₂, Pd/BaSO₄, Quinoline (Lindlar's catalyst)) cis-2-butene

2-butyne

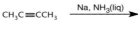

$CH_3C{\equiv}CCH_3$ →(Na, NH₃(liq)) trans-2-butene

2-butyne

Free radical addition

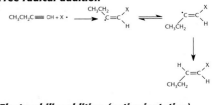

Electrophilic addition (anti orientation)

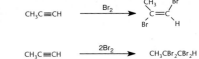

$CH_3C{\equiv}CH$ →(Br₂)

$CH_3C{\equiv}CH$ →(2Br₂) $CH_3CBr_2CBr_2H$

Hydroboration (cis alkene formed)

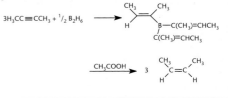

$3H_3CC{\equiv}CCH_3 + \frac{1}{2} B_2H_6$ →

→(CH₃COOH) 3

ALKENES

Cis isomers have higher boiling points than trans isomers due to its net dipole moment. Trans isomers have higher melting points than cis isomers due to more effective arrangement, more efficient packing.

Catalytic Reduction

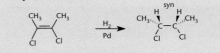

Electrophilic Addition of HX

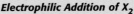

Electrophilic Addition of X_2

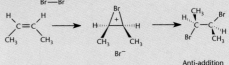

Anti-addition

Electrophilic Addition of H_2O

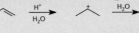

Free Radical Addition (anti-Markovnikov)

most stable radical

Hydroboration (anti-Markovnikov, syn orientation)

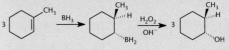

Oxidation with $KMnO_4$

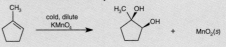

Oxidation with O_3

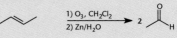

AROMATIC COMPOUNDS

Cyclic, conjugated polyenes that possess $4n + 2$ π electrons (Huckel's Rule) and adopt planar conformations to maximize overlap of π orbitals are aromatic. Aromatic compounds are fairly unreactive because of stabilization of delocalized π electrons.

Aliphatic compounds are all compounds that are not aromatic.

Antiaromatic compounds are cyclic, conjugated polyenes with $4n$ π electrons.

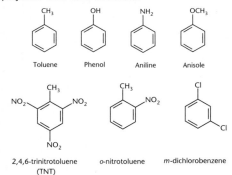

Toluene   Phenol   Aniline   Anisole

2,4,6-trinitrotoluene (TNT)   o-nitrotoluene   m-dichlorobenzene

p-methylbenzoic acid

ALCOHOLS

- Higher boiling points than alkanes
- Weakly acidic hydroxyl hydrogen

Synthesis

- Addition of water to double bonds
- S_N1 and S_N2 reactions
- Reduction of carboxylic acids, aldehydes, ketones and esters
  - aldehydes and ketones with $NaBH_4$
  - esters and carboxylic acids with $LiAlH_4$

Reactions

E1 dehydration reactions in strongly acidic solutions

Hoffman product   minor

Zaitsev product   major

Substitution reactions after protonation or leaving group conversion

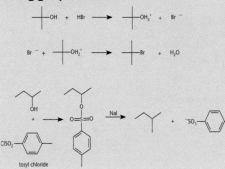

tosyl chloride

Catalytic Reduction

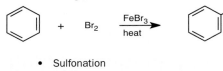

Electrophilic Aromatic Substitution

- Halogenation

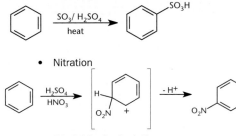

- Sulfonation
- Nitration
- Friedel-Crafts Acylation

DIRECTING SUBSTITUENTS

Activating ortho/para	Deactivating ortho/para	Deactivating meta
NH_2, NR_2, OH, NHCOR, OR, OCOR, and R	F, Cl, Br, I	NO_2, SO_3H, COOH, COOR, COR, CHO

Oxidation

- PCC takes a primary alcohol to an aldehyde

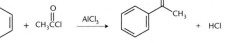

- Jones's reagent, $KMnO_4$, and alkali dichromate salts will convert secondary alcohols to ketones and primary alcohols to carboxylic acids

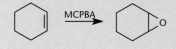

- Tertiary alcohols cannot be oxidized without breaking a carbon to carbon bond

Oxidation and reduction

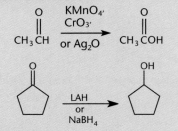

Wittig Reaction

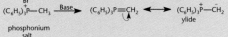

phosphonium salt   ylide

ETHERS

Ethers are only very slightly polar; with no hydrogen bonding, they boil at temperatures close to comparable alkanes. They are only slightly soluble in water and can be easily hydrolyzed with water.

Synthesis

Williamson Ether synthesis

Internal S_N2 displacement to form a cyclic ether

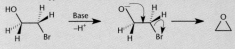

Peroxy acid and alkene form an oxirane

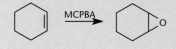

MCPBA

Reactions

- Form peroxides upon reaction with oxygen in the air
- Cleavage with HBr or HI and high temperature
- Acid- and base-catalyzed ring opening of epoxides

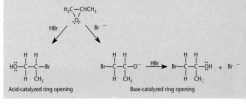

Acid-catalyzed ring opening   Base-catalyzed ring opening

ALDEHYDES

The dipole moment of aldehydes causes an elevation of boiling point, but not as high as alcohols since there is no hydrogen bonding.

Synthesis

- Oxidation of primary alcohols
- Ozonolysis of alkenes
- Friedel–Crafts acylation

Reactions

Reactions of Enols (Michael additions)

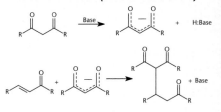

Nucleophilic addition to a carbonyl

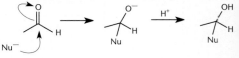

Aldol condensation

An aldehyde acts both as nucleophile (enol form) and target (keto form)

CARBOXYLIC ACIDS

Carboxylic acids have pKa's of around 4.5 due to resonance stabilization of the conjugate base. Electronegative atoms increase acidity with inductive effects. Boiling point is higher than alcohols because of the ability to form two hydrogen bonds.

Synthesis
Oxidation of primary alcohols with $KMnO_4$

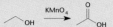

Organometallic reagents with CO_2 (Grignard)

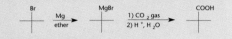

Hydrolysis of Nitriles

Reactions
Formation of soap by reacting carboxylic acids with NaOH; arrange in micelles

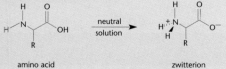

nonpolar tail   polar head

Nucleophilic acyl substitution
- Ester formation
- Acyl halide formation
- Reduction to alcohols

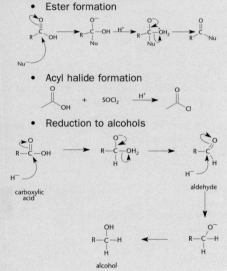

AMINO ACIDS, PEPTIDES, & PROTEINS

Amino acids have four substituents: amine group, carboxyl group, hydrogen, and R group. Amino acids are **amphoteric**—they can act as either acids or bases and often take the form of **zwitterions** (dipolar ions).

amino acid   zwitterion

Structure
Primary: sequence of amino acids

Secondary: α-helix, β-pleated sheet

Tertiary: disulfide bridges, hydrophobic/hydrophilic interactions

Quaternary: arrangement of polypeptides

Henderson–Hasselbalch Equation

$pH = pK_a + \log$ [conj. base]/[conj. acid]

CARBOXYLIC ACID DERIVATIVES

Acyl halides
Nucleophilic acyl substitution

Friedel–Crafts acylation

Reduction

Anhydrides
Synthesis via reaction of carboxylic acid with an acid chloride

Hydrolysis
Conversion into esters and carboxylic acids
Addition of ammonia to form amides

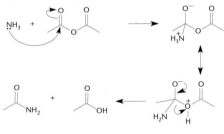

Friedel–Crafts acylation

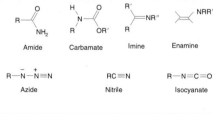

Amines & Nitrogen Containing Compounds

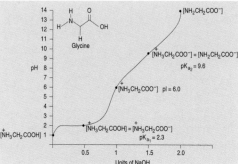

Amide   Carbamate   Imine   Enamine

Azide   Nitrile   Isocyanate

Direct alkylation of ammonia

Reduction from nitro compounds, nitriles, imines, and amides

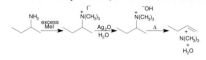

Exhaustive methylation (Hoffman elimination)

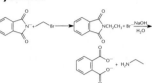

Gabriel Synthesis

Amides
Synthesis via reaction of acid chlorides with amines or acid anhydrides with ammonia

Hydrolysis
Hoffman rearrangement converts amides to primary amines

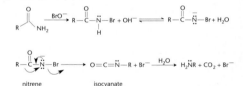

nitrene   isocyanate

Reduction with LAH

Esters
Synthesis via condensation of carboxylic acids and alcohols

Hydrolysis in acid or base
Conversion to amides

Transesterification
Grignard addition
Claisen Condensation

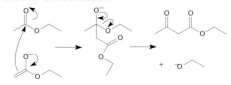

Reduction

PURIFICATION METHODS

Extraction separates dissolved substances based on differential solubility in aqueous vs. organic solvents.

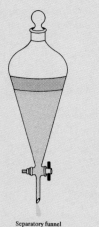

Separatory funnel

Filtration separates solids from liquids.

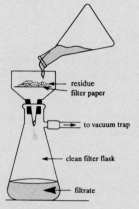

residue
filter paper

to vacuum trap

clean filter flask

filtrate

Vacuum filtration

Chromatography uses a stationary phase and a mobile phase to separate compounds based on polarity and/or size.

solvent front

$R_f = \frac{X}{Y}$

Thin-layer chromatograms

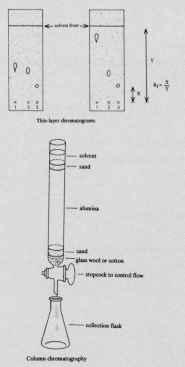

solvent
sand

alumina

sand
glass wool or cotton
stopcock to control flow

collection flask

Column chromatography

Sublimation separates solids based on their ability to sublime.

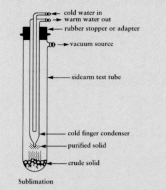

cold water in
warm water out
rubber stopper or adapter

vacuum source

sidearm test tube

cold finger condenser
purified solid
crude solid

Sublimation

Centrifugation separates large particles based on mass and density.

armored chamber

rotor

sedimented sample

drive motor   Centrifuge

Distillation separates liquids based on boiling point, which depends on intermolecular forces. Types are simple, fractional and vacuum.

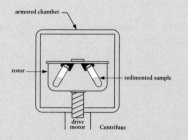

thermometer

condenser

vacuum adapter

clamp

water outlet
water inlet
distilling flask

to vacuum source
clamp

receiving flask

heat source

ice bath

Vacuum distillation

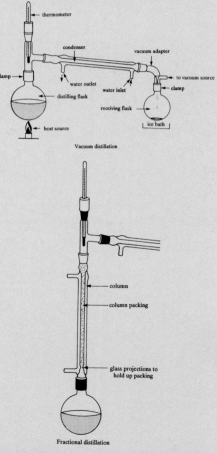

column

column packing

glass projections to
hold up packing

Fractional distillation

Recrystallization separates solids based on differential solubility in varying temperatures.

Electrophoresis is used to separate biological macromolecules based on size and/or charge.

SPECTROSCOPY

Infrared Spectroscopy measures molecular vibrations of characteristic functional groups.

Functional Group	Frequency (cm^{-1})	Vibration
Alkanes	2800 — 3000	C—H
	1200	C—C
Alkenes	3080 — 3140	=C—H
	1645	C=C
Alkynes	2200	C≡C
	3300	≡C—H
Aromatic	2900 — 3100	C—H
	1475 — 1625	C—C
Alcohols	3100 — 3500	O—H (broad)
Ethers	1050 — 1150	C—O
Aldehydes	2700 — 2900	(O)C—H
	1725 — 1750	C=O
Ketones	1700 — 1750	C=O
Acids	1700 — 1750	C=O
	2900 — 3300	O—H (broad)
Amines	3100 — 3500	N—H (sharp)

UV Spectroscopy involves passing ultraviolet light through a chemical sample and plotting absorbance versus wavelength. It is most useful for studying compounds containing double bonds and/or heteroatoms with lone pairs.

Mass Spectrometry uses a beam of electrons to ionize a sample, and then measures deflection of accelerated particles in a magnetic field. Ultimately, the mass/charge ratio is plotted against relative abundance and mass is extrapolated. It provides molecular weight of compounds.

^{1}H NMR and ^{13}C NMR are two forms of **Nuclear Magnetic Resonance**.

^{1}H NMR Chemical Shifts	
Type of Proton	Approximate Chemical Shift δ (ppm) Downfield from TMS
RCH$_3$	0.9
RCH$_2$	1.25
R$_3$CH	1.5
–CH=CH	4.6–6
–C≡CH	2–3
Ar–H	6–8.5
–CHX	2–4.5
–CHOH/–CHOR	3.4–4
RCHO	9–10
RCHCO–	2–2.5
–CHCOOH/–CHCOOR	2–2.6
–CHOH–CH$_2$OH	1–5.5
ArOH	4–12
–COOH	10.5–12
–NH$_2$	1–5

CARBOHYDRATES

Monosaccharides are the simplest carbohydrate unit and are classified by the number of carbons they possess. D and L designations: if the lowest -OH is on the left, the molecule is L. If the -OH is on the right, it's D.

Straight chain monosaccharides such as glucose can convert to a cyclic form.

ENZYMES

- Protein catalysts that are not consumed or changed (exception is ribozymes)
- Reduce the activation energy but do not affect the overall free energy
- Optimal conditions for most human enzymes: $T = 37°C$, pH = 7.4

KINETICS

- When [substrate] is low compared to [enzyme], many active sites are empty
- Increasing [substrate] increases the rate up until V_{max} is reached.

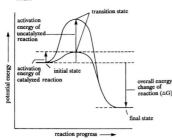

Reaction Coordinate

THE CELL

FLUID MOSAIC MODEL AND MEMBRANE TRAFFIC

- Phospholipid bilayer with cholesterol and embedded proteins
- Exterior hydrophilic phosphoric acid region
- Interior hydrophobic fatty acid region

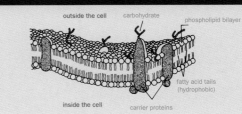

REGULATION

- **Allosteric:** binding of an effector molecule at allosteric site.
- **Feedback inhibition:** end product inhibits an initial enzyme pathway
- **Reversible inhibition:** competitive inhibitors bind to active site; noncompetitive inhibitors to the allosteric site

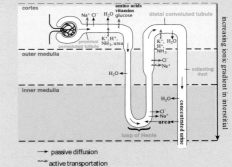

HOMEOSTASIS

Kidneys regulate [salt] and [water] in the blood. Its functional unit is the nephron.

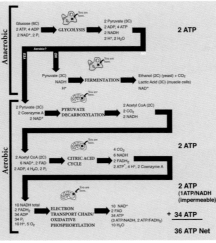

→ passive diffusion
⇝ active transportation

OSMOREGULATION

- **Filtration** at the glomerulus. Filtrate (fluid and small solutes) passes through. *Passive*
- **Secretion** of acids, bases, and ions from interstitial fluid to filtrate. Maintains pH, [K^+] and [waste]. *Passive and Active*
- **Reabsorption:** essential substances and water flow from filtrate to blood. Enabled by osmolarity gradient and selective permeability of the walls. *Passive and Active*

HORMONAL REGULATION

Aldosterone

- stimulates Na^+ reabsorption and K^+ secretion, increasing water reabsorption, blood volume and blood pressure
- secreted from adrenal cortex
- is regulated by renin-angiotensin system

ADH

- increasing collecting duct's permeability to water to increase water reabsorption
- is secreted from posterior pituitary with high [solute] in the blood

THE LIVER'S ROLES IN HOMEOSTASIS

1. gluconeogenesis
2. processing of nitrogenous wastes (urea)
3. detoxification of wastes/chemicals/drugs
4. storage of iron and vitamin B_{12}
5. synthesis of bile and blood proteins
6. beta-oxidation of fatty acids to ketones
7. interconversion of carbs, fats, and amino acids

GLUCOSE CATABOLISM

Glycolysis occurs in the cell cytoplasm: $C_6H_{12}O_6 + 2ADP + 2P_i + 2NAD^+ \rightarrow$ 2 Pyruvate + 2ATP + 2NADH + $2H^+ + 2H_2O$.

Fermentation occurs in anaerobic conditions. Pyruvate is converted into lactic acid (in muscle) or ethanol (in yeast).

Respiration occurs in aerobic conditions.

- **Pyruvate decarboxylation:** Pyruvate converted to acetyl CoA in the mitochondrial matrix.
- **Citric acid cycle:** Acetyl CoA enters, NADH, $FADH_2$, CO_2 produced.
- **Electron transport chain:** Coenzymes are oxidized, and energy is released as electrons are transferred from carrier to carrier.
- **Oxidative phosphorylation:** Electrochemical gradient caused by NADH and $FADH_2$ oxidation provides energy for ATP synthase to phosphorylate ADP into ATP.

REPRODUCTION

CELL DIVISION

- G_1: cell doubles its organelles and cytoplasm
- S: DNA replication
- G_2: same as G_1
- M: the cell divides in two
- Mitosis = PMAT
- Meiosis = PMAT × 2

Mitosis

Meiosis

SEXUAL REPRODUCTION

Meiosis I:

- Two pairs of sister chromatids form tetrads during prophase I.
- Crossing over leads to genetic recombination in prophase I.

Meiosis II:

- Identical to mitosis, but no replication.
- Meiosis occurs in **spermatogenesis** (sperm formation) and **oogenesis** (egg formation).

FOUR STAGES OF EARLY DEVELOPMENT

cleavage: mitotic divisions
implantation: embryo implants during blastulation
gastrulation: ectoderm, endoderm, and mesoderm form
neurulation: germ layers develop a nervous system

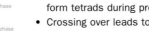

Ectoderm "Attract-o-derm"	Nervous system, epidermis, lens of eye, inner ear
Endoderm "Endernal" organs	Lining of digestive tract, lungs, liver and pancreas
Mesoderm "Means-o-derm"	Muscles, skeleton, circulatory system, gonads, kidney

ENDOCRINE SYSTEM

Direct hormones directly stimulate organs, tropic hormones stimulate other glands.
Mechanisms of hormone action: **peptides** act via secondary messengers and **steroids** act via a hormone/receptor binding to DNA. Amino acid derivatives may do either.

Hormone	Source	Action
Follicle-stimulating (FSH)	Anterior pituitary	Stimulates follicle maturation; spermatogenesis
Luteinizing (LH)		Stimulates ovulation; testosterone synthesis
Adrenocorticotropic (ACTH)		Stimulates adrenal cortex to make and secrete glucocorticoids
Thyroid-stimulating (TSH)		Stimulates the thyroid to produce thyroid hormones
Prolactin		Stimulates milk production and secretion
Endorphins		Inhibit the perception of pain in the brain
Growth hormone		Stimulates bone and muscle growth/lipolysis
Oxytocin	Hypothalamus; stored in posterior pituitary	Stimulates uterine contractions during labor, milk secretion during lactation
Vasopressin (ADH)		Stimulates water reabsorption in kidneys
Thyroid hormones (T_4, T_3)	Thyroid	Stimulates metabolic activity
Calcitonin		Decreases (tones down) blood calcium level
Parathyroid hormone	Parathyroid	Increases the blood calcium level
Glucocorticoids	Adrenal cortex	Increases blood glucose level and decreases protein synthesis
Mineralocorticoids		Increases water reabsorption in kidneys
Epinephrine, Norepinephrine	Adrenal medulla	Increases blood glucose level and heart rate
Glucagon	Pancreas	Stimulates conversion of glycogen to glucose in the liver, increases blood glucose
Insulin		Lowers blood glucose, increases glycogen stores
Somatostatin		Supresses secretion of glucagon and insulin
Testosterone	Testes	Maintains male secondary sexual characteristics
Estrogen	Ovary/Placenta	Maintains female secondary sexual characteristics
Progesterone		Promotes growth/maintenance of endometrium
Melatonin	Pineal	Unclear in humans
Atrial natriuretic peptide	Heart	Involved in osmoregulation and vasodilation
Thymosin	Thymus	Stimulates T lymphocyte development

FOUR STAGES OF MENSTRUAL CYCLE:

(1) Follicular: FSH causes growth of a follicle
(2) Ovulation: LH causes follicle to release egg
(3) Luteal: corpus luteum forms
(4) Menstruation: endometrial lining sheds

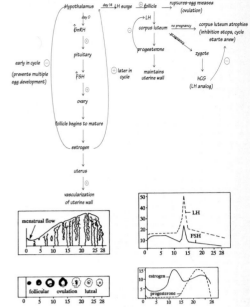

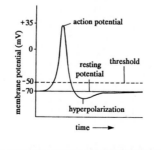

MUSCULOSKELETAL SYSTEM

Sarcomere
- contractile unit of the fibers in skeletal muscle
- contains thin actin and thick myosin filaments

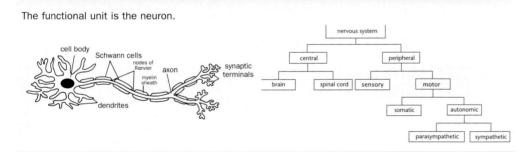

CONTRACTION

Initiation:
- Depolarization of a neuron leads to action potential.

Sarcomere shortening:
- Sarcoplasmic reticulum releases Ca^{2+}.
- Ca^{2+} binds to troponin on the actin filament.
- Tropomyosin shifts, exposing myosin-binding sites.
- Myosin binds, and ATPase activity allows myosin to pull thin filaments towards the center of the H zone and then ATP causes dissociation.

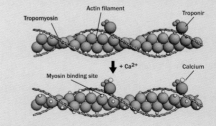

Relaxation:
- Ca^{2+} is pumped back into the sarcoplasmic reticulum.

BONE FORMATION AND REMODELLING
- **Osteoblasts**: builds bone
- **Osteoclasts**: breaks down bone
- **Reformation**: inorganic ions are absorbed from the blood for use in bone
- **Degradation (Resorption)**: inorganic ions are released into the blood

NERVOUS SYSTEM

The functional unit is the neuron.

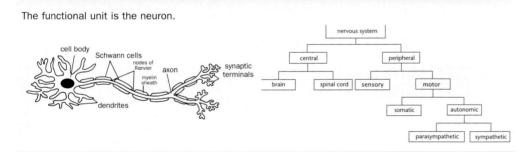

Resting potential:
- 3 Na^+ pumped out for every 2 K^+ pumped in.

Action potential:
- Stimulus acts on the neuron, depolarizing the membrane of cell body

Impulse propagation:
- Depolarization (Na^+ rushing into axon) followed by repolarization (K^+ rushing out of axon) along the nerve axon

The synapse:
- At the synaptic knob, voltage-gated Ca^{2+} channels open, sending Ca^{2+} into the cell.
- Vesicles fuse with presynaptic membrane sending the neurotransmitter across the **synapse**.
- It binds to receptors on the postsynaptic membrane, triggers depolarization of next cell.

ACTION POTENTIAL

I	Rest	All gates closed
II	Depolarization	Na^+ gates open
III	Repolarization	Na^+ gates close
		K^+ gates open
IV	Hyperpolarization	All gates closed

CIRCULATION

CIRCULATORY PATHWAY THROUGH HEART

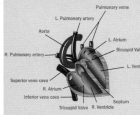

superior and inferior vena cava → right atrium → right ventricle → pulmonary artery → lungs→ pulmonary vein → left atrium → left ventricle → aorta → body

3 Portal systems: blood travels through an extra capillary bed before returning to the heart:
- Liver (hepatic), kidney, and brain (hypophyseal).

FETAL CIRCULATION
- **Foramen ovale:** connects right and left atria.
- **Ductus arteriosus:** connects the pulmonary artery to aorta. Along with foramen ovale, shunts blood away from the lungs.
- **Ductus venosus:** connects umbilical vein to inferior vena cava, connecting umbilical circulation to central circulation.

BLOOD COMPONENTS

Plasma: aqueous mix of nutrients, wastes, hormones, blood proteins, gases and salts.

Erythrocytes (red blood cells): carry oxygen
- Hemoglobin: 4 subunits carry O_2 and CO_2. Iron controls binding and releasing.
- Oxygen-hemoglobin dissociation:

Factors leading to right shift of curve:
- ↑ Temperature
- **Bohr Effect**
  - ↓ pH, ↑ P_{CO_2}
  - O_2 release to tissues enhanced when H^+ allosterically binds to Hb. ↑ P_{CO_2} leads to ↑ [H^+]:

$$CO_2 + H_2O \underset{\text{carbonic anhydrase}}{\rightleftharpoons} H_2CO_3 \rightleftharpoons H^+ + HCO_3^-$$

Leukocytes (white blood cells): function in immunity

Platelets: clotting
- release thromboplastin, which (along with cofactors calcium and vitamin K) converts inactive prothrombin to active thrombin
- thrombin converts fibrinogen into fibrin, which surround blood cells to form the clot

BLOOD TYPING

Antigens are located on the surface of red blood cells

Blood type	RBC antigen	Antibodies	Donates to:	Receives From:
A	A	Anti-B	A, AB	A, O
B	B	Anti-A	B, AB	B, O
AB	A, B	None	AB only	All
O	None	Anti-A, B	All	O

Blood cells with Rh factor are Rh^+ and produce no antibody. Rh^- lack antigen and produce an antibody.

RESPIRATION

GAS EXCHANGE
- occurs across the thin walls of **alveoli**.
- deoxygenated blood enters the pulmonary capillaries that surround the alveoli.
- O_2 from the inhaled air diffuses down its gradient into the capillaries, where it binds with hemoglobin and returns to the heart.
- CO_2 from the tissues diffuses from the capillaries to the alveoli, and is exhaled.

FETAL RESPIRATION
- Fetal hemoglobin has a higher affinity for oxygen than adult hemoglobin.
- Gas and nutrient exchanges occur across the placenta.

DIGESTION

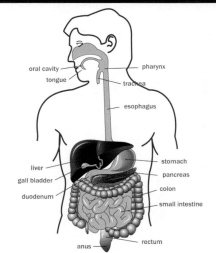

CARBOHYDRATE DIGESTION

Enzyme	Site of Production	Site of Function	Hydrolysis Reaction
Salivary amylase (ptyalin)	Salivary glands	Mouth	Starch → maltose
Pancreatic amylase	Pancreas	Small intestine	Starch → maltose
Maltase	Intestinal glands	Small intestine	Maltose → 2 glucoses
Sucrase	Intestinal glands	Small intestine	Sucrose → glucose, fructose
Lactase	Intestinal glands	Small intestine	Lactose → glucose, galactose

PROTEIN DIGESTION

Enzyme	Production Site	Function Site	Function
Pepsin	Gastric glands (chief cells)	Stomach	Hydrolyzes specific peptide bonds
Trypsin	Pancreas	Small Intestine	Hydrolyzes specific peptide bonds. Converts chymotrypsinogen to chymotrypsin
Chymotrypsin			Hydrolyzes specific peptide bonds
Carboxypeptidase			Hydrolyzes terminal peptide bond at carboxyl
Aminopeptidase	Intestinal glands		Hydrolyzes terminal peptide bond at amino
Dipeptidases			Hydrolyzes pairs of amino acids
Enterokinase			Converts trypsinogen to trypsin

IMMUNE SYSTEM

- The body distinguishes between "self" and "nonself" (antigens)

HUMORAL IMMUNITY (specific defense)

B lymphocytes

memory cells remember antigen, speed up secondary response → **plasma cells** make and release antibodies (**IgG, IgA, IgM, IgD, IgE**), which induce antigen phagocytosis

- **Active immunity:** antibodies are produced during an immune response.
- **Passive immunity:** antibodies produced by one organism are transferred to another organism.

CELL-MEDIATED IMMUNITY

T lymphocytes

cytotoxic T cells destroy cells directly

suppressor cells regulate B and T cells to decrease anti-antigen activity

helper T cells activate B and T cells and macrophages by secreting lymphokines

memory cells

NONSPECIFIC IMMUNE RESPONSE

Includes skin, passages lined with cilia, macrophages, inflammatory response, and interferons (proteins that help prevent the spread of a virus).

LYMPHATIC SYSTEM
- lymph vessels meet at the thoracic duct in the upper chest and neck, draining into the veins of the cardiovascular system.
- vessels carry **lymph** (excess interstitial fluid), and capillaries (**lacteals**) collect fats by absorbing chylomicrons in the small intestine.
- **lymph nodes** are swellings along the vessels with phagocytic cells (leukocytes) that remove foreign particles from lymph.

LIPID DIGESTION
- When chyme is present, the duodenum secretes CCK (cholecystokinin) hormone into the blood.
- CCK stimulates the secretion of pancreatic enzymes and bile.
- Bile is made in the liver and emulsifies fat in the small intestine; it's not an enzyme.
- Lipase is an enzyme made in the pancreas that hydrolyzes lipids in the small intestine.

CLASSICAL GENETICS

- If both parents are Rr, the alleles separate to give a genotypic ratio of 1:2:1 and a phenotypic ratio of 3:1.

Law of independent assortment: Alleles of unlinked genes assort independently in meiosis.

- For two traits: AaBb parents will produce AB, Ab, aB, and ab gametes.
- The phenotypic ratio for this cross is 9:3:3:1.

STATISTICAL CALCULATIONS

- The probability of producing a genotype that requires multiple events to occur equals the *product* of the probability of each event.
- The probability of producing a genotype that can be the result of multiple events equals the *sum* of each probability.

GENETIC MAPPING

- Crossing over during meiosis I can unlink genes (Prophase I).
- Genes are most likely unlinked when far apart.
- One "map" unit is 1% recombinant frequency.

Given recombination frequencies

X and Y: 8%
X and Z: 12%
Y and Z: 4%

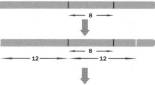

INHERITED DISORDERS in PEDIGREES

- Autosomal recessive: skips generations
- Autosomal dominant: appears in every generation
- X-linked (sex-linked): no male-to-male transmission, and more males are affected.

EVOLUTION

- When frequencies are stable, the population is in **Hardy-Weinberg equilibrium**: no mutations, large population, random mating, no net migration, and equal reproductive success.

$$p + q = 1; \quad p^2 + 2pq + q^2 = 1$$

p = freq. of dom. allele q = freq. of rec. allele
p^2 = freq of dom homozygotes
$2pq$ = freq of heterozygotes
q^2 = freq of recessive homozygotes

MOLECULAR GENETICS

NUCLEIC ACID

- Basic unit: nucleotide (sugar, nitrogenous base, phosphate)
- DNA's sugar: deoxyribose. RNA's sugar: ribose.
- 2 types of bases: double-ringed purines (adenine, guanine) and single-ringed pyrimidines (cytosine, thymine, uracil).
- DNA double helix: antiparallel strands joined by base pairs (A=T, G≡C).
- RNA is usually single-stranded: A pairs with U, not T.

TRANSCRIPTION REGULATION, PROKARYOTES

Regulated by the **operon**:
- structural genes: have DNA that codes for protein
- operator gene: repressor binding site
- promoter gene: RNA polymerase's 1st binding site
- Inducible systems need an inducer for transcription to occur. Repressible systems need a corepressor to inhibit transcription.

MUTATIONS

- **Point**: one nucleotide is substituted by another; they are silent if the sequence doesn't change.
- **Frameshift**: insertions or deletions shift reading frame. Protein doesn't form, or is nonfunctional.

VIRUSES

- acellular structures of double or single-stranded DNA or RNA in a protein coat.
- Lytic cycle: virus kills the host.
- Lysogenic cycle: virus enters host genome.

DNA REPLICATION

- **Semiconservative:** each new helix has an intact strand from the parent helix and a newly synthesized strand.

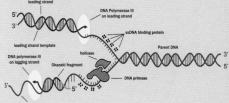

EUKARYOTIC PROTEIN SYNTHESIS

- **Transcription**: RNA polymerase synthesizes hnRNA using a DNA, "antisense strand" as a template.
- **Post-transcriptional processing**: introns are cut out of hnRNA, exons spliced to form mRNA.
- **Translation:** occurs on ribosomes in the cytoplasm.

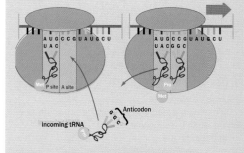

- **Post-translational modifications:** (i.e., disulfide bonds) made before the polypeptide becomes a functional protein.

DATA ANALYSIS

A researcher performed the following experiments in order to investigate the metabolism of two different strains of bacteria, Strain 1 and Strain 2.

Experiment 1

Strains 1 and 2 were incubated in separate broth cultures for 24 hours at 37° C. A sample of each culture was streaked onto three different plates—A, B, and C—each containing a different starch-agar medium; the plates were then incubated for another 48 hours at 37°C. The plates were then examined for surface colony growth and stained with iodine solution to determine the extent of starch digestion.

Table 1

	Surface colony growth			Starch digestion		
	A	B	C	A	B	C
Strain 1	+	+	+	–	–	–
Strain 2	+	+	–	+	+	–

key: + = growth; – = no growth

Experiment 2

The two strains were incubated in the same manner as in Experiment 1. Two 100-mL portions of agar were poured into two beakers, which were maintained at 43°C. Next, 0.2 mL of broth culture from Strain 1 was pipetted into the first beaker, and 0.2 mL of broth culture from Strain 2 was pipetted into the second beaker. The agar was swirled around to distribute the bacteria evenly through the media, and then poured onto plates. These plates were incubated for 48 hours at 37°C and then examined for colony growth both on the agar surface and lower down within the oxygen-poor agar layer.

Table 2

	Surface colony growth	Deep-agar colony growth
Strain 1	+	–
Strain 2	+	+

key: + = growth; – = no growth

Once incubated, bacteria will grow if nutrients they can metabolize are available. Keep this in mind as you interpret the procedure and results.

Experiment 1 and Table 1: What are the important aspects? **Two strains** (1 and 2) undergo **identical incubation on 3 plates with different starch agars.** Look at Table 1, one strain at a time. The researcher observes growth and starch digestion. Strain 1 grows on all plates, but doesn't digest the starch: it must be using another nutrient to grow. We don't know that Strain 1 *can't* digest starch—we just know that it's not digesting it in the first 48 hours. Strain 2 uses starch to grow on plates A and B, but doesn't digest starch or grow on plate C. Again, we don't know that Strain 2 *can't* digest the starch in medium C—we just know it's not in the first 48 hours.

Experiment 2 and Table 2: Note the significant differences between the two experiments. This time, the strains were **separately** distributed **within the agar** instead of jointly streaked on top of multiple agars. The researcher observes growth on top and within, the assumption being that the top is oxygen-rich and within is oxygen-poor. What does it mean that Strain 1 only grows in an oxygen rich environment? It is an obligate aerobe that requires oxygen for metabolism. What does it mean that Strain 2 can grow in oxygen rich *and* oxygen poor environments? It is a facultative anaerobe.